THE NOTORIOUS GIG

A CREATIVE GUIDE TO GETTING IN GOOD
AS A FREELANCER.

ANTHONY Q. ROBERTS

Cover and interior pages by Johari Huggins

Published by 83 Ink
5540 Centerview Dr. Ste. 204
PMB 132948
Raleigh, NC 27606-8012

TheNotoriousGIG.com

ISBN: 978-0-9859210-8-8

Library of Congress Control Number: 2023911738

To Johari and Onyx, you are my inspirations.

To my big homie, Parde. Forever grateful for the blueprint.

To Tombol and Funmi…we still reminisce over you.

CONTENTS

PREFACE

I WAS WRITING A BOOK & THEN...

2020

Like a lot of people, I was chilling in February of 2020. I was working as a freelance creative, raising my son with my wife and just generally trying to figure out my next move. I started writing this book and began going back and forth in my head about whether or not I wanted to continue. I believed in the idea and thought that people could benefit from knowing some of the basics of freelancing, but I honestly didn't know if I wanted to put the effort and energy into a book project. I was doing well in the freelance space myself so I wasn't in need of money and I was just generally unsure if this was what I wanted to do.

And then in March everything changed.

I watched the news like you and saw the millions of people who were now out of work because of the pandemic. I heard the stories of people attempting to find new normals, new ways to support themselves and their families. Stories of trying to regain some sense of financial assurance and stability in one of the most unstable periods that we've ever lived through. I knew some of these people personally, worked with others and can empathize with all of them, knowing first hand how it feels to pivot when you're not expecting it. When my career as a journalist that I'd worked so hard for was jeopardized by the Great Recession starting in '08, I also had to make a move. So I get it (more on that later).

HAPPENED

In this book are some of the ways I made that move and still continue to implement these principles in my career today. What started out as a pivot grew into a privilege, turning a freelance hustle into a full-time career.

So in a certain sense, the pandemic forced my hand, but it pushed it towards you. It highlighted how important this book could potentially be to people, to families and to careers. I felt the need was even greater than I thought when I first started writing it, and that was the push that I needed to finish it and offer it to you. I feel good about the fact that this may be a life raft to someone, a second chance to someone else, or a launching pad into a completely new field for another person.

However you choose to use what's in this book, be sure to define a vision for yourself and use these tools in the service of that vision. That's all I ask. Thank you for spending time with this book. I hope it leads you towards your vision.

INTRODUCTION

AYE LISTEN, I KNOW WE JUST MET

But let's just consider ourselves friends. Because that's the best way to do this. Which means that what I'm about to give you isn't advice, it's just a conversation with a friend about freelancing. Because conversation is a bridge to understanding and people take recommendations from friends, not so much from people they don't know. And so you can't say that you don't know me, let me let you in on a little of my background, friend.

When I first started as a freelancer, I was still in college and determined to be a music journalist. I had made this decision years ago, on the floor of my room, or riding the train or wherever I was as I poured over stacks and stacks of magazines growing up. I bought them every month and devoured them from cover to cover, reading every page, feature, album review and cover story. I even made some questionable fashion choices from getting suckered by the ads in the magazines.

Back then, publications like *The Source*, *XXL*, *VIBE* and a host of others were speaking to my friends and I in a language that we spoke too, the language of hip hop culture. I saw myself in those pages and wanted to contribute to the culture that inspired me so much by documenting it through the eyes of someone who both lived and loved it. There was nothing else I really wanted to do at the time.

That was my dream.

I went firmly and confidently in the direction of that dream. I started off by going to the library and reading whatever I could find about getting published in a magazine. I was there all the time, looking up stuff on the internet, and when my internet time was up (you only got 60 minutes per session) I went back to the books on the shelves to see what else I could find. This was how I learned about what a masthead was.

After that, I started looking up the names of editors in the mastheads of the magazines I was reading and awkwardly emailing them, trying to start a conversation. I was trying to let them know who I was and why I needed to be in their pages. I emailed them for any reason I could, just to stay top of mind (and possibly top of the trash folder, too.) I pitched story ideas and sometimes fully written pieces, trying to get my foot in the door. I heard no after no after no after… you get the point.

Basically, it wasn't working out. Most of those magazines were in New York, and here I was a kid from Chicago with no way to get face time (before there was FaceTime) with anybody who could give me a yes. But I was persistent, emailing many of the editors weekly for what seemed like forever before eventually getting a few yes's from a few small circulation magazines and websites. And even though I got a certain satisfaction, a certain early validation from starting to get a few clips and freelance assignments, I wasn't getting paid.

—

So here I was pursuing my dream, but still in my grandma's house. It wasn't coming together fast enough. I had to get a job at a certain package handling company and felt salty the whole time I was there. I felt like I wasn't supposed to be there. I was a writer, but writing wasn't helping me chip in on the bills, so I called myself paying dues. I didn't have the knowledge at the time that I could essentially expand my dream. That expansion was made possible by the first Ad Man I'd ever known, Parde Bridgett.

Being a fellow Chicagoan, hip hop head and writer himself, after we were introduced by one of my former high school teachers, Parde and I immediately started building a rapport. We emailed back and forth with darted language, the result of two writers feeling each other out. And after showing him a few pieces I was writing at the time on spec and looking to get published, it turned into him mentoring me; giving feedback, constructive criticism and ways to make the writing better.

After a few months, he said rather leisurely in passing "Hey, if you ever want to try your hand at the advertising/marketing game, let me know."

Let you know???
What???
Hell yeah!!!

I jumped at the chance. At the time, I only knew that advertising meant tv commercials and print ads. I had seen so many print ads in the pages of those magazines every month and thought to myself, "I could write that better," not ever thinking I would get a chance to.

Parde was a Creative Director and essentially took me under his wing. He gave me the game on how to structure and refine my writing to the medium of advertising. This essentially opened up another avenue to utilize my craft, all while still trying to get my bylines in the big magazines. At that time, you couldn't have told me that the ad stuff I was doing on the side, basically to fund my real dream, would turn into a seperate, successful career for me later down the line.

After a few years of flipping no's into yes's and becoming what I would call a successful freelance journalist, I like a lot of other people got blindsided. A lot of the magazines I was writing for, that I had grown up on and others I had grown to love, were facing something they hadn't seen before. Basically all of these outlets started to either cut back dramatically or disappear completely off of newstands.

This was circa 2008 and the so-called "Great Recession" was doing a number on millions of people across the country, and my little corner of the world was no different. I went from having assignments and gigs coming weekly to not even monthly. And even the work I was getting was for way less than even just a year prior. Magazines were my bread and butter, the lion's share of my income. It was also the career that I had put so much into and endured years of no's to create, but here it was, shrinking right in front of my eyes. The industry as a lot of us knew it was shifting. A new wave was coming and threatened to wash a lot of people out with the tide. If there was ever a sink or swim moment, this was it.

I was in a jam to say the least and wasn't sure what I was going to do. By this time I was out on my own and I had to make something happen because rent doesn't pay itself. I had the ad game itch and had been freelancing in the marketing and advertising space ever since Parde put me on, so when things got rocky in the magazine world, I turned my freelance ad work into full-time ad work. It was a pivot that was desperately needed and one I was extremely grateful for.

I saw a lot of my friends, peers and colleagues struggle to either make ends meet or figure out what their next career move was going to be. I saw the confidence melt from people's faces at the prospect of losing their livelihoods. I saw otherwise smart and capable people become stagnant in the face of uncertainty, and for that reason alone I wrote this, hoping that it might help prevent you from being stuck or unstick yourself if you need to, on your own terms.

Having the flexibility to maneuver into another industry that had only been an afterthought for so long was eye opening. It opened me up to recognizing more possibilities and seeing the value in keeping your career options open. I went from being a writer/journalist covering music, culture and fashion to being a writer in the ad world, creating work for brands like Nike, Facebook, adidas, Sony, Gatorade, Kawasaki and a bunch of others.

And while I've had full-time posts at both magazines and ad agencies, 10+ years of my career has been freelance. Even when I had full-time jobs, I never stopped freelancing. I never wanted to lose the muscle, because it had taken me so far in both of my careers.

Here we are again, facing something else we haven't seen before. People have lost their jobs in the millions, and I've once again seen friends and colleagues scramble to figure out what to do next. Which tells me that what I'm offering is valuable. If not for now, then for later.

In my career(s) I've learned a lot, mostly through trial and error, things that might be helpful to you as you ride this freelance wave. So that's what I'm offering, a few suggestions from a friend that can help you develop a skill set that can get you in good, no matter where you choose to take it.

Even before COVID, 35% of the American workforce were freelancers. As many have lost their jobs, even more people have forcibly become freelancers as we navigate a new normal across the board. Whether you're looking to freelance full-time, make extra money on the side, stay afloat while you figure out what's next or just not live in fear of being fired, you came to the right spot.

THIS IS THE TIME TO GET IN GOOD.

A FEW NUMBERS TO THROW AT YOU:

70%

OF FREELANCERS **SAY IT TOOK LESS THAN A YEAR TO EARN MORE** WHILE FREELANCING **VS. THEIR PREVIOUS EMPLOYMENT**

59M

PEOPLE WORKED AS **FREELANCERS IN 2021**

65% OF FREELANCERS EXPECT THEIR **INCOME TO INCREASE** IN THE COMING YEAR.

Upwork's *Freelance Forward: 2022* Independent Workforce Report

IT'S ABOUT FINDING *YOUR* LANE.

PART 1: **BEFORE THE GIG**

PRACTICE MAKES PERFECT... FOR YOU

Like meditation or medicine, band rehearsal or law, freelance is a practice.

IT'S not a hard and fast way of being. If anything, it's the opposite. Freelancing, especially in the creative industries, requires you to be nimble, flexible, at-the-ready and willing to shift according to the situation. What you will find in this book are some of the ways I built my practice, and some fundamentals to help you build yours.

My hope is that you take these tools and build a foundation that works for *you*.

While this book is for those looking to start freelancing and get that notoriously tough first freelance gig, those using freelance to transition into a new field will also benefit from these lessons, as they will resonate with anyone at any point in their freelance journey. Sometimes remembering some of the basics I learned in year one has helped me get through gigs more than ten years later. The point is the information will always be valuable, and hopefully you can take this and add to it.

CHAPTER 1

YOUR FIRST CHECK: A REALITY CHECK

Throughout my career, my primary goal has always been to do good work. My secondary goal was to make money. And sometimes the order of those switched. Let's be real, mortgages, rent and other living expenses don't wait for that perfect gig that utilizes all your skill sets. Sometimes you have to take a gig, or two, or probably more, that don't necessarily excite you. That's just the reality. But the beauty in that reality is that taking those gigs keeps you in the game. So that when that perfect gig that utilizes all your skill sets does come along, you're able to take it.

There were a lot of times earlier in my career that I had misplaced feelings towards a gig. It wouldn't necessarily be what I was clamoring to do, so I would villainize it, poke holes in it, complain about it, blah blah blah. I later learned, though, to properly appreciate those gigs. They kept my rent paid, utilities on and boots off my cars, which allowed me to continue forging a career path on my terms. *That* was more important to me than anything.

Even when I took a full-time agency position, it was always on my terms because I always knew that if I needed to, I could go back to freelancing. I was never afraid of getting fired because I had developed a skill set that would help me, at the least, tread water until my next move.

So to be clear, there will be shitty gigs, working with or for shitty people, having to chase down your checks and a million other things you'll run into as a freelancer. Those are some of the realities that come along with this sometimes. The key is to put these things into proper perspective.

Sometimes, there's no stopping it and you have no control of how a gig goes. It may turn out that you thought you were signing up for one thing and it turns out to be something completely different. That will happen, too. But there is a way for those to be more the outlier situations than your constant experience.

I learned way back in high school journalism class the who, what, where, when, why and how of reporting. Since you're a freelancer, and are essentially reporting to yourself, asking yourself some key questions and giving honest answers can help you create the environment to land that first gig, and a first gig you actually want.

Asking these questions has saved me from a bunch of headaches, a gang of curse words, more than a few bogus projects and a tall number of regrets. So I thought I'd offer up a few to you as well. Use these as a base and then ask yourself some deeper questions, ones that only you would know to ask.

LET'S START WITH WHO...

WHO ?

Who are you working with?

Let me say this very clearly, a lot of freelancing is who you know. But if you're just getting into this, you may not know anybody yet. That's cool, don't trip. That just means you need to start getting to know people. Sometimes it could be worth it to take a gig that might pay a little less or might not be the most exciting project if who you're working with can make up for it.

Networking, recommendations and reputation plays a big part in this. Showing what you can do or forging relationships with other creatives and decision makers is a way to play the long game. I'm not saying be phony, I'm not saying be fake. I'm a card carrying member of the Sometimes Anti Social Club, so I get it. But be willing to make thoughtful and genuine connections that are a win for you both. How you choose to do it is up to you.

Who's gonna see this?

If you're looking to switch gears a little bit and go from say, sports to fashion, it will help to get pieces for your portfolio that may help you get more gigs in that field. Having the audience you're trying to reach in mind when considering whether to take a gig can help you make an informed decision. You know that old saying about dress for the job you want not the one you have? Yup, same thing here.

WHAT ?

What are you working on?

Is it something you love, like, tolerate or hate? Being real about your feelings about a project could help you know whether to take it or take a pass.

What do you have to lose or gain?

More plainly stated, what's on the line here? Is your rent due? Will this project take time away from something else? Is your name attached to this? It's essentially just a reframing of the pros and cons, but framing it as what you have to lose or gain may help you put the gig into better context. If you think about it like a hike, will you lose or gain footing from this. Whatever you do, watch your step.

What's driving you?

Understanding, remembering and using your reason(s) why you're getting into freelance can be a great compass when trying to figure out which direction you should be going in. These "know yourself" types of questions are crucial to building a career based on your individual wants and needs, so spend some time getting familiar with your driving forces. They may be clear (i.e. extra income) or some may be a little bit deeper (like wanting to prove to yourself you can

WHERE ?

succeed at something new). Whatever they are, spend time with them and carry them with you as you proceed.

Where are you now?

Understanding where you are in your personal, professional and financial life at the moment can be crucial to knowing where your motivations or roadblocks might be. People have told me they would start freelancing if they didn't just buy a house, or if they had more saved up, or some want to start so they can reach a quick money goal. Sitting with yourself and evaluating your current "location" in this moment in time is the type of self awareness you need to healthily and not haphazardly step into this freelance thing. There's no judgment, you're ready when you're ready, and when you are, knowing these answers will be key.

Where are your strengths and where can you improve?

I'm not even a big list type of guy, but this one needs to be listed out. By hand. There's a different level of tangibility that comes from doing things by hand, especially writing, and grounding yourself in these tangible realities are big. This needs to be a super honest list, as it will be a guide to knowing if a gig is for you or not. It will also help you to understand what assets you are bringing to the table immediately and what areas you need to work on and work through. You'll need to not only know this yourself but be able to communicate it to others, so get as clear here as possible.

WHEN?

When are you going to have another chance at this?

Freelance is usually some combination of good fortune, good contacts, good work and good timing. The latter is one you should consider when looking at a gig. An opportunity may present itself that may not come around again and those are the ones you need to jump on. With the quickness. But be real with yourself, if you're just hoping that this is an opportunity that it might not be, you can end up saying yes to some mess.

When is enough enough?

Or in more plain terms, what's your limit? This is another way you can gauge if a gig is or isn't for you. For example, there are places I've freelanced where I have a great time, get along great with everyone and usually do great work. These usually happen during shorter gigs. Sometimes those same places will hit me up for longer gigs that I have to respectfully decline. I know that if I was at these places any longer than say two months, the bottom would fall out. We'd get on each other's nerves, the paint would peel and the curtain would be drawn. So I stay swimming in the shallow end of the pool with these companies, make a big splash, and everybody floats along happily. You too should know your threshold.

WHY?

Why are you doing this?

This is possibly the most important one. Is it for the money? Is it to work on a particular brand, to try to gain experience in a particular area? This is the thing that you will always come back to. For motivation, solace, confirmation and more. Being clear with yourself and others about why you're doing this, in the larger sense, should be a prerequisite question before you take the gig. Any gig. Should I say it a little louder for the people in the back?

Why should anyone hire you?

Is it because you're highly skilled? Is it because you're a people person? Is it because you're a great leader? Are you actually the best person for this or someone who will do? Knowing why (or if) you should be hired also helps you know how to show up, how to approach and how to ultimately succeed on a gig or project. It'll help guide you through a lot of your decisions in your freelance journey so spend a good amount of time on this one.

HOW ?

How can this help you?

Quick story, one of my full-time agency jobs earlier in my career had me writing dozens of direct mail pieces (postcards) and several formulaic radio spots every week. It was tedious, sometimes creatively numbing and I thought it was essentially a waste of my time.

Seeing my distaste, the senior writer took me to lunch and basically said, "Hey, I know this isn't the sexiest job, but trust me, after doing this you'll be one of the quickest, most efficient writers out there." I didn't believe him, too stuck in my own ideas and displeasure for the job.

About a year later, I left and landed at another agency. When I got there, I realized I finished my projects faster than all the other writers, having put in the hours and mental muscle memory penning hundreds of postcards. When I went back into freelancing, my quickness and clarity became one of my strongest assets and landed me a lot of work. Point is, freelancers need a set of skills and tools. They might not always come to you nice and shiny, but if you're open they'll help you with the nuts and bolts of this thing.

So ask yourself, how can this gig help me?

PREP YOURSELF

BEFORE YOU WRECK YOURSELF

A GOOD PREP TALK

So what do you do with the answers to these questions? You give yourself an honest and inspiring Prep Talk. It's like a regular pep talk, but one that proves you're ready to get into freelancing.

A prep talk can help you go in understanding what you're doing, where you are in your journey and some initial boundaries you may want to put in place. It can also help you feel confident about passing on an opportunity if you decide it's not right for you, instead of mourning over the "loss" of a gig.

Grounding yourself in this proof by writing it down, by hand, and saying/reading it to yourself whenever you need a reminder can really help. Why? Because a lot of what holds people back from freelance is not that they aren't capable or qualified, it's because they may not believe that they are. On the next page I put together a quick example format of a bare bones Prep Talk that you can use as a tool and fill in with your own answers. Remember, this is you developing your practice. Use this tool to get charged, get excited, get clear and get in good.

PREP TALK EXAMPLE:

ACCEPT

If I take this gig, I'd be working with a good friend on a social media campaign for a local business.

I'm in a place where I could use the cash.

I'm willing to work for a couple of weeks but I'm not willing to go much longer than that and put a strain on our friendship.

I want to get more social work in my portfolio so I can get more gigs in that space and I also want to make a little extra money.

So I'm deciding to ***book*** the gig.

And being clear on my reasons, I feel good about moving in this direction.
Let's get it!

PREP TALK EXAMPLE:

DECLINE

If I take this gig, I'd be working with an old boss I don't really care for on a campaign pitch for a national brand.

I'm in a place where I'm okay in terms of money so it's not really about the cash.

I'm willing to work four weeks but I'm not willing to extend any longer.

I want national brands in my portfolio
and I also want this work to get produced
but there are no guarantees it will.

So I'm deciding to
pass on the gig.

And being clear on my reasons, I feel good
about moving in this direction. ***On to the next.***

TRUE... AND ALSO TRUE.

There are a lot of notions about freelance that some people may see as positive and others may see as negative. It's my experience that this binary of negative and positive doesn't really fit what it means to be freelance. So as a believer in multiple truths, I've expanded it to be a representation of not "two sides" but instead "more sides" to what comes with this path.

These ten simple truths represent income, fulfillment, time off, work culture and income again because well, money's important. This list could go on for pages and pages, but these ten are symbolic of some of the core ways you may need to shift the way you perceive work. Freelance is about flexibility. Keeping these things in mind can be a good stretching exercise.

This is True	**This is Also True**
Make More Money	Incur More Expenses
More Control of Your Projects	More Looking For Your Projects
Take Leave Anytime	Pay Your Own Leave
No Office Drama	No Office Parties
Bigger Checks	Waiting For/Chasing Checks

CHAPTER 2

WHAT'S YOUR HOOK?

What distinguishes you in the sea of freelancers?

Recruiters, editors, creative directors, or whoever in your industry that can hire you needs to understand who you are and what you're offering. Establishing an identity as a freelancer is a great way to increase the likelihood of getting booked and booked for the gigs you actually want.

Remember you are your business and every successful business has a business model. While sometimes it may look like a free-for-all out there, the freelancers that are the most in demand are usually the ones who understand what piece of the pie they're going for and how to show up to get it.

On the following pages we'll get into some creative archetypes you can use, dissect, combine, try on, whatever you need to do to figure out what kind of freelancer you want to be. The goal is to look at these and see yourself in one of them. Or a couple of them. And if you don't see yourself in any, then you at least now have the foundation of knowing you need to create your own.

THE SPECIALIST

You've put a lot of time and effort into a particular industry (i.e. sports, hospitality, fashion, etc) and you want to either work on projects in that field exclusively or at least have it be the lion's share of your work. If this is you, you've already got a leg up on other freelancers, but you still have to translate that experience into gigs. A specialist can carve a nice niche for themselves if they can demonstrate the practical value of their experience.

A lot of industries move fast, with new innovations happening all the time that change the shape and face of that industry. This means you don't want to oversell your past experience, but instead find a nice balance between showcasing what you've done and demonstrating how that helps you now. That industry might shift, change or even gets away from some of the areas that you've put time into, but the knowledge you've gained about the goals of that industry will always be valuable.

I had years of experience in the magazine industry, but a lot of the magazines I wrote for are no longer around. The thing that I was an expert in was storytelling. It didn't matter if it was a magazine article, a billboard or a TV commercial, storytelling is always the common thread. So be sure to know where the root of your expertise lies so that you can properly leverage that into consistent gigs, even when the techniques and tactics of an industry change.

Experience

Versatility

Collaborative

Resourceful

THE MOTTO:

"I AIN'T NEW TO THIS, I'M TRUE TO THIS."

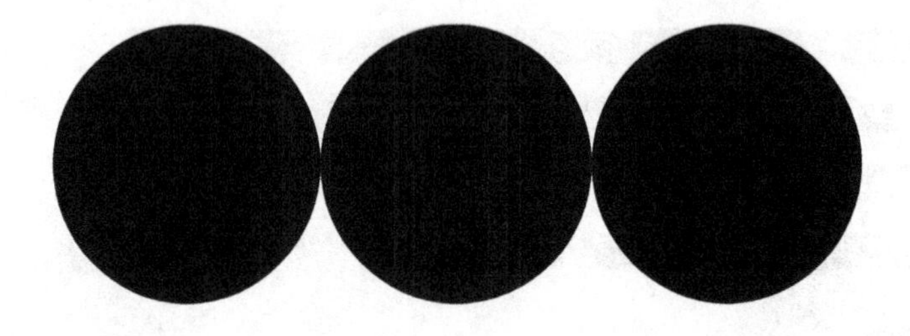

THE ROLE PLAYER

This is gonna be the person that keeps their head down and gets the work done. I can't tell you how valuable this person is to a project and the overall morale of the group you're working with. They usually take feedback well, which is by no means a given, and don't bring a lot of ego to their work. They're altruistic and highly collaborative. They don't need the hand-holding because they're more of a self starter.

There's not a lot of glory in this one, unless you count continually counting checks as glorious. But you do need to be honest with yourself. This one isn't for everybody, especially if you're trying to get a little more shine or recognition on the projects you work on. There's nothing wrong with wanting to get props, just know that this may not be the way to do that.

Dependability is one of the best traits that a freelancer can have, and the Role Player is nothing if not dependable. You're essentially behind the scenes, but as many professionals will tell you, those behind the scenes are usually the ones with the longest careers.

Experience

Versatility

Collaborative

Resourceful

THE MOTTO:

"I GET IN WHERE I FIT IN."

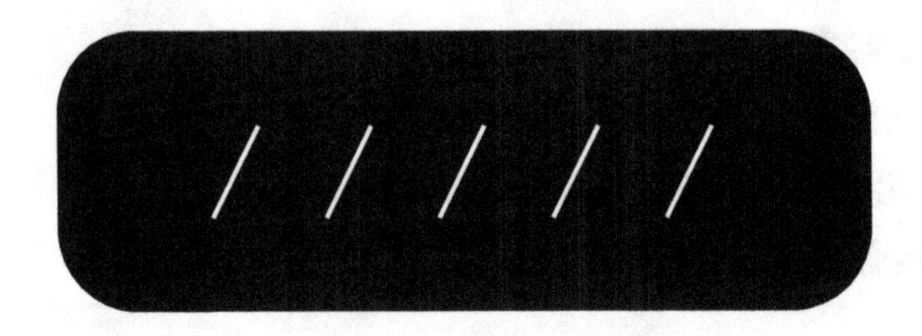

THE SLASHER

This is that hodge-podge, creative collage type of person. Someone who's highly adaptable and usually able to take on a variety of projects and assignments because of their eclectic background. They usually have a larger collection of skill sets (think painter/coder/production artist/designer) that may not perfectly fit into just one description.

They're able to jump in and hit the ground running immediately because they have a good set of fundamental skills that can be applied to multiple asks. If you've spent time doing "odd jobs," or being a Jack/Jill-of-All-Trades, this can be a sweet spot for you.

You can also choose to silo or focus on a particular skill set if a gig calls for just one thing, but relaying your multi-faceted background as a whole can work well, too. Those with eclectic and varied interests or those able to quickly re-frame things do well in this spot. They are highly coveted because of their wider breadth of experience, in a similar way that the Specialist is valued for their depth of experience.

Experience

Versatility

Collaborative

Resourceful

THE MOTTO:

"I DO A LITTLE BIT OF EVERYTHING."

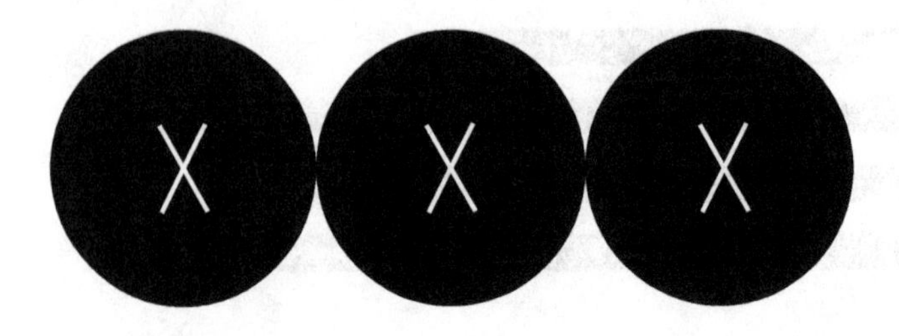

THE FIXER

Usually for the more experienced. Someone you call at the "last minute" with the tight deadline. This one calls for a person who is cool under pressure, may (or may not) have a calming demeanor and understands that they are being brought in to save asses.

This person may not get the same regularity of gigs that some others do, but because of their highly coveted ability to right the ship, they can also charge more for their services which could essentially make up the difference. This can also be a fit for those who are comfortable in their full-time gig, but have a lot of experience that they could bring to a situation given the right circumstances.

Experience

Versatility

Collaborative

Resourceful

THE MOTTO:

"I'VE SEEN THIS BEFORE."

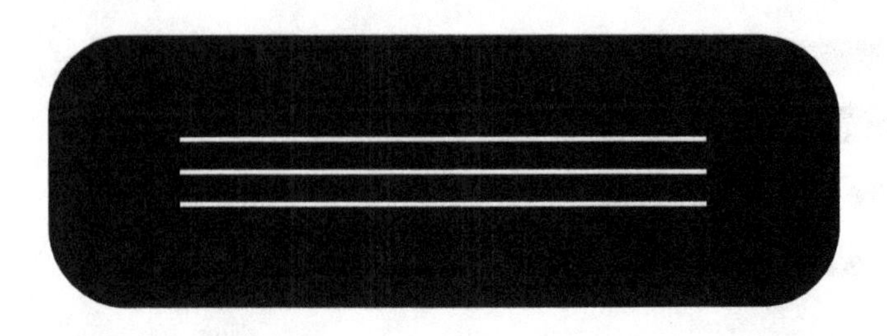

THE CHECK CHASER

Don't let the name fool you, this isn't necessarily bad. This is just a person who is very clear that they are there for the money. They don't care about the politics, they're not auditioning for a full-time spot, they don't need to be invited to the office party. They just need that Net-30 to not spill over into 31.

This archetype will quickly learn one of the cornerstones of freelancing; knowing who pays on time. This is something that you'll come to make note of as you move forward in your practice, and if you're like me, you may even base your decision to take a gig or not on it.

This person might also get called for those not-so-sexy gigs that some might pass on, but if you're just in it for the cash, that works. Letting people know where your priorities lie can put you in line for a steady line of work, and those checks can start to look very sexy. This may also be a good potential archetype for short-term freelancers.

Experience

Versatility

Collaborative

Resourceful

THE MOTTO:

"I JUST WANT THE BREAD."

THE TUNNEL VISIONARY

Another approach that may work for you could be honing in on a particular sector of the freelance market. Putting your efforts towards a focused area like big brands, start ups or tech companies is a good way to build a reputation as a freelancer.

Before I had big brand experience, I initially made a name for myself with start-ups. The focused approach made me desirable to a community that shared contacts and resources. It was a good way to learn the ropes while on the gig and was a great way to collaborate as a true partner, as many start ups are looking for your expertise to help them build from scratch.

While it may not seem as glamorous, there's a lot of opportunity in working exclusively or almost exclusively on small brands as well. You often get to be a lot more creative and take more risks, as a lot of small brands are usually looking for unique and innovative ways to make their mark.

It also helps if you've either had a small business/start up yourself or spent time working at one of these brands, but not a necessity.

Experience

Versatility

Collaborative

Resourceful

THE MOTTO:

"I KNOW WHERE MY BREAD IS BUTTERED."

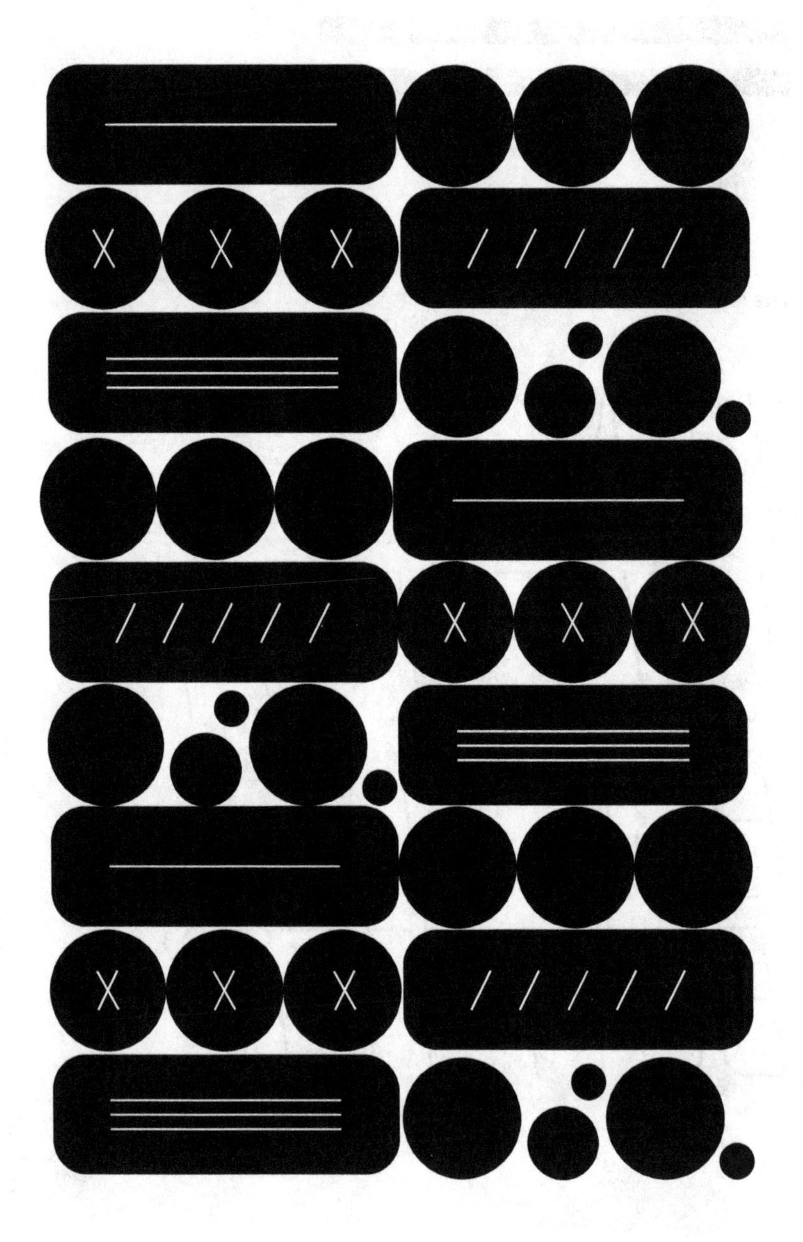

THE PORTFOLIO

Hopefully you can see yourself as one of these archetypes. Or if not, maybe they've given you something to think about as far as what you do want your archetype to be. No matter which one(s) you choose you'll need to have a portfolio that reflects this. Below you'll find the type of work examples to include on your website.

–

Elements of unique insight or talent
You need to show your thinking and ability. Whether in project descriptions, how you present the work... it's up to you. Get me into your head so you can be on my mind.

Work displaying various or specific skills
You can't expect anyone to know what you can do, you define that narrative. You can call yourself as many things (i.e. writer/designer/producer/vocalist) as you'd like, but you'll most likely only be getting booked for as many things as you can show.

Work that's current
You don't need to automatically replace your favorite or most successful projects if they were a little while ago, but remembering to continue adding new work is key. It shows you not only have done great work, but are doing great work.

A FEW THINGS TO KEEP IN MIND:

ABC (Always Be Campaigning)

Before you have a steady roster of clients or consistent opportunities coming your way, your job is to build your reputation. Let people know what you do, even people not in that field. I would have never met the person that introduced me to advertising if it wasn't for one of my former teachers, who knew I was a writer, introducing us. The takeaway; a lot of freelancing is who you know, but also who knows you.

Find A Partner

Whether it's a writer/art director pairing, stylist/MUA, find someone with a complimentary skill set that you can make things with. You can always market your individual services, but having the added advantage of packaging your talents can be good for both of you. Just make sure you know their work, work ethic and working style, though, as they can be a reflection on you and your reputation.

Stay Out Of The Politics

Wherever you freelance, whether in-office, on-site or remote, know that every place comes with its own hierarchy and politics. *Don't get involved in that shit!* One of the best parts about freelance is that you don't have to get roped into the energy suck that is the politics of a place. Keep your head down, keep your nose clean and don't bother with all the extras.

CHAPTER 3

BUILDING RELATIONSHIPS

Every business must build relationships; as a freelancer you are your business.

A restaurant has to build a relationship with its customers, right? They also have to build a separate relationship with its suppliers. And another relationship with its staff, and so on and so on. You see where I'm going?

You need to be able to do this too, building different types of relationships at various levels. Each will have different nuances, factors and functions. But please believe, this is a key part of being successful as a freelancer.

You also will need to be able to build multiple micro-relationships with the scores of people that you will be working with. This isn't easy for a lot of people, so I'll give you some of the ways that have worked for me until you find your own rhythm.

RELATIONSHIPS VS. CONTACTS

First, it's important that we establish the difference between a relationship and a contact. Both are necessary, but they are not inherently the same. A contact is someone in the same field/industry or an adjacent industry that you do business with. It's strictly transactional. I call you when I need something, you call me when you need something. It's understood. We're good for each other's business so we keep doing business together.

A relationship can also be business, but there's a different level of investment. It's not only business. I know something about you, you know things about me. We've broken bread, we don't hit each other up just when something is needed. We don't have to be best friends or kick it on the weekends, but there's more of a personal connection there.

Cool? Cool. Now that we got that out the way, lets keep going.

THERE ARE MORE BENDS THAN STRAIGHT LINES IN THIS FREELANCE THING.

YOU'RE GONNA NEED TO BORROW MORE THAN A CUP OR TWO OF SUGAR FROM YOUR NEIGHBORS IF YOU'RE GONNA MAKE IT IN THIS NEIGHBORHOOD.

SO BEING A GOOD NEIGHBOR YOURSELF, IS HOW YOU BUILD A HEALTHY, FUNCTIONING COMMUNITY.

FEEL ME?

COFFEE DATES ARE STILL UNDEFEATED

One of the best ways to get contacts as well as build relationships is the tried and true coffee date. Its a low-pressure way to introduce yourself and get to know people you could potentially be doing business with. We live in a time where a lot of communication and work is done virtually, and whenever an in-person coffee date can't happen, a virtual one can.

The point is to get face time, and whether in person or virtually, it's invaluable when you're in the getting-to-know-you phase.

Oh, and don't expect every coffee date to result in a gig. As a matter of fact, a lot of them won't. Some won't immediately but may down the line. Some will just be a formality to getting the gig. Some will just be practice. Your goal should be to get some on the calendar and let everyone know who you are and what you're looking to do.

Who should you be getting coffee with? Recruiters, creative directors, business owners, fellow freelancers, you name it. Anyone who may be able to help you and that you may be able to help, too.

PRACTICE THE ART OF

WORKING TOGETHER.

5 TIPS ON BUILDING CREATIVE SYNERGY

Freelance requires you to work with new people literally all the time, which is a gift and a "cursive" opportunity. I say cursive because it'll put you through loops sometimes, but when its done it can be a beautiful outcome. You need to be able to develop at the very least a working rapport and at best real synergy to make the best work possible.

This may not be a strength for you now, but don't let that deter you. It's a skill that can be developed, and even though this isn't the space to go into that in detail, I want to offer a few tips to get you started that can help you begin the practice of building quick and genuine working relationships.

1:

Ask About Their Process

Understanding how a person likes to work is half the battle. It tells you where their comfort zone is and how they prefer to get things done. Having a baseline knowledge of what makes a person feel at their best is essential to knowing what will ultimately produce the best work.

Asking about the ways in which they have and have not collaborated is key as well. There are so many options and scenarios that allow for collaborating that you may or may not be used to the same things. Don't assume, get clear on this and keep it in mind as you either work or consider working together.

2:

Let Them Know How You Like to Work

Clearly communicating how you like to work is also a big part of this. Instead of just being agreeable and saying "however you like to work is fine" tell people your preferences. It can still be a "however you like to work" type of situation if that genuinely suits you, but giving where you are upfront helps people know the same things about you that you're trying to learn about them.

So much of this is a matter of give and take, and giving your own process credit and validity is a great way to take some of the guesswork out of the upfront of this relationship.

3:

Closed Minds Don't Get Fed

Be willing to learn new ways of thinking, new ways of working, and new ways of thinking about work. Take what you've learned from them, as well as your own processes and try to identify the common denominators first. Beginning with the commonalities is a great way to develop a foundation with that person or team and creates a clear starting point.

After that, flexibility is key. Yes, learning new programs, systems, platforms and formats can come with a certain amount of stress or uncertainty, but remember that this is not just about you, and understand that you are adding valuable knowledge and skills to your freelance toolkit as well.

4:

Free For Lunch?

Sharing a meal, a slice of pizza or some other food or drink is one of the best ways to quickly build a rapport. But sit down, though.That's how it works best. There is a certain amount of professional intimacy that comes with this, and it's another great set up for that foundational connection. Ideating, being vulnerable when sharing ideas, navigating issues and problem solving all are intimate acts.

If you can't do it in person, do it virtually. The biggest part of this is actively listening and actively sharing. So if face-to-face is not an option, face-to-screen can be a back-up. Just remember to not constantly look at yourself during the virtual calls. Preoccupation with how you look means less presence which also means less connection.

5:

Put Yourself in Their Shoes

What does it take to do their job?

What drives them?

What challenges could they be facing that you may be unaware of ?

These are a few questions to start off, as putting yourself in the other person's shoes is critical. It will help you develop a certain care and understanding that is essential for healthy creative relationships. These aren't the only questions to ask, but starting with these can take you down a good path to gaining much needed perspective and empathy with your potential creative partner.

ONE LAST THING...

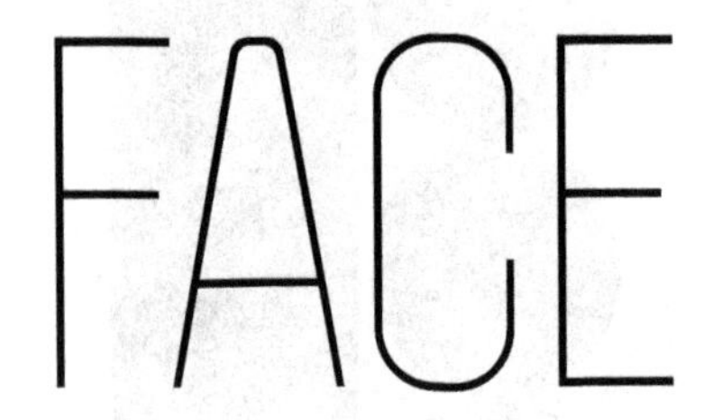

I completely understand the uncertainty.

The imposter syndrome.

The risks.

The ups and downs.

Trust me. I get it.

YOUR FEAR.

But when freelancing, you need to face those fears, accept them, and move forward. Hell, use them as motivation. Whatever you need to do. Because if you don't move past these things, you run an even bigger risk.

Making fear-based decisions.

Nothing will stall you more than making fear-based decisions. This freelance path is made much more clear with a clear head and clear conscious.

PART 2: **DURING THE GIG**

YOU FINALLY GOT IT. NOW LET'S GET IT.

Congratufuckinglations!!!

This is a moment. An accomplishment. A huge win. It's the whole point that you got this book and that you started this journey in the first place. You should take a moment to pump your fist, shout, breakdance, whatever.

You deserve it. But literally, this is when the work starts.

So don't slack up. Now you need to make sure that you do everything in your power to make this successful. You've already put in a good amount of work, but freelance is an active sport. Your target tends to keep moving, so that means you keep moving. That means being a perpetual participant in your own prosperity.

CHAPTER 4:

TO-DO FOR DAY ONE

Okay, now you're in there. Great. The next part of the process involves you observing, advocating and executing. A good freelancer is always aware of their surroundings. In order to be at peace with your environment (no matter how chaotic that environment might possibly be) you need to take note of how this living organism of a project works. Also, knowing how the place where you will be working works will be key, too.

You'll also need to advocate for yourself. Remember, it is ultimately up to you to put yourself in the best position possible, so being diligent about or even creating a process that involves advocacy will be important. Both your observation as well as advocacy should be in the service of execution. These are critical components of doing your job and doing it well.

QUESTION EVERY THING

Ask Your Ass Off

When someone hires you for a gig, they're hiring you for a specific role. It's your responsibility to ask questions about that role and what comes with it, as it can change from project to project and place to place.

Sometimes a client is clear on what they want, complete with a brief, goals and objectives laid out. In that case, my job is just to execute on those goals. Other times a client has no idea what they want and they are hiring me to help them figure it out. These are two very different gigs. Getting clear about what a client is looking for and what they are asking you to do could be the difference between success and failure.

I know the feeling of being so excited that someone wants to hire you that you just want to jump at the opportunity feet first. Been there, done that. Trust me, even if you're trying to "not f*ck it up" you still need to know what you're getting into for everybody's sake, especially yours. It's a good idea to get your role and responsibility clearly stated in your contract so that both you and who's hiring you are on the same page about what your output, contribution, performance and collaboration should look like. That's how you go into it *head* first.

OFFICE INS AND OUTS

SOME THINGS TO THINK ABOUT IN-OFFICE:

Climate

As a freelancer you'll be working with a variety of places that all have their own way of doing things. There's relationships, power dynamics and histories that you'll be walking into at every place. Some places will be more quiet, work independently type of places. Others may be loud and collaborative. Some may be modern and progressive and others more traditional or even behind the times. Limber up and be flexible to adjust and adapt to your working environment.

Title Differences

Be sure that you understand what the title differences are as you go from place to place. Depending on where you are, a 'producer' could be a person that facilitates shoots, manages a digital project or makes beats. That's a wild range. Get to know the lingo wherever you go.

Decision Makers

Knowing who can give you a 'no' or a 'yes' answer is very important. Creatively, knowing who's in charge matters as well. Freelancers are often given directions and input from multiple people on a project. Knowing how to properly prioritize that feedback is crucial, and that comes from identifying the decision makers. Also, know who can bring you back after a project is done. Is it the CD? The recruiter? Making sure that person understands the value you bring is key to getting repeat gigs.

SOME THINGS TO THINK ABOUT OUT-OF-OFFICE:

Clocking Hours

If you're in-office you're probably keeping and tracking hours on that office's platform. Out in the wild, you need to track your own. It's important to do them daily so you don't forget, which is very easy to do. Also be honest. You can ruin a relationship over a few dollars by inflating hours. You'll make much more money in the long run with the truth. That also means be honest with yourself, too. If you did the mental labor of thinking/concepting/ideating for three hours and sat down for 30 minutes to physically write those ideas out, you've worked 3.5 hours.

Flexible Workspace

Freelancers have always needed to be flexible with the way that we work. From quickly adapting to various office spaces to moving from one coffee shop to another, we can sometimes find ourselves in the shuffle of places and spaces to work. That can be a daunting reality, especially for those that crave a sense of consistency or grounding in order to do their best work.

I've found that making yourself a N.O.T.E., or Needed Objects To Execute, is key. These are essentially your must-haves for creating the kind of working environment that you need. Identifying these things, and making sure that you have them whether you're in your living room or in a conference room, means that you become less dependent on an actual place to work but instead shift your perspective on what helps you perform at your best.

These can be photos of family, your own computer or drawing tablet, music, or any number of things that help you work best. Identifying these things and bringing them with you, no matter where you are, can help to make anywhere work for you.

DON'T JUST LEARN YOUR LINES IN THE PLAY.

LEARN THE WHOLE SCRIPT.

KNOW YOUR ROLES

Freelancing, no matter what field you're in, is inherently collaborative. In one way or another, you're usually working with a team, even if your part of the job may be siloed. There's someone who is before and after you in the process of seeing a project through. So not only should you not make their jobs harder, understanding those jobs could possibly make both of your jobs easier. And who doesn't continually hire someone who makes their job easier?

If you're looking to go above and beyond, which is a good way to distance yourself from the rest of the pack, you should know everyone else's role as well.

CHAPTER 5

MONEY MATTERS

The word freelancing is inherently misleading, because this ain't supposed to be free, at least not permanently. This is about you having a particular set of skills, talent, acumen, know-how, experience and ability which is deservant of compensation. As I said in the beginning of the book, I wasn't getting paid when I started and for a while I was okay with that. I felt like I had things that I needed to improve and clips I needed to get. But the goal wasn't to do pro-bono for the long haul.

I know that navigating the money side of things can be tricky. Instead of trying to cover everything about such a vast and nuanced topic, I'm sticking to some of the basics that helped me build my practice. I'll share some of the ways I've charted the money waters and I'll tap some "freelance" help to explain the rest. I know a lot of freelancers who all have different approaches and philosophies on money, so the point is to help you develop a point of view on money that feels right and respectful to you and your work.

CREATING YOUR RATE

As I've progressed in my career, I have asked and been asked about how to charge for freelance services. This still seems to be a touchy subject for a lot of people, and I get it. You might not want to charge $$$ because it might turn people off. You might not want to charge $ because people may not take you seriously. You might not want to be aggressive in asking for your money because it might make that client not want to work with you again. You might not want to be meek in asking for your money because you might not get it. And you might not this. And you might not that.

The real might, or strength in money matters, is knowing what matters to you.

I've felt all of these, and a bunch more, and you probably will too. So I'm not going to tell you what you should be charging. Instead, I'll help you understand a few ways that you can come to a rate that you can feel comfortable with.

So let me break this 'don't talk about what you make" taboo a little bit and start by telling you a little about where I started.

As a freelance journalist, like I said before, I started at Free.99. I was okay with that because the name of the game at that time was getting into a print magazine. This was before the full digital revolution and many online publications weren't paying. Glossy mags were still the standard. Whatever I felt would get me closer to that, I was with it. It helped me understand the process of writing for magazines, lead times, how interviews were coordinated, who the contact people were and other valuable things that were forming my knowledge base in the business of magazines.

—

When I started freelancing in advertising, I started at $25 an hour. I had no idea what to charge when they asked me and when they said "how bout $25 an hour," I took it immediately. That was more than all my friends were making. I didn't know people made this much to write, and even though I didn't have an exact number in my mind before the offer, starting for free like I'd done before wasn't an option anymore. I had decided that my goal was to be good enough to make this reliable income.

I share these two very different approaches I took to demonstrate that knowing what you are in this for is key when dealing with money.

A FEW KEY FACTORS TO CONSIDER WHEN DETERMINING YOUR RATE:

LEVEL OF EXPERIENCE

This is usually thought of in years, and some will tell you that there are certain skills and tricks-of-the-trade that only come with time. This is true. I can personally vouch for this, as parts of my career could have only been developed through maturity and dedication to process. But with that said, years aren't the only way to gauge or validate your experience.

In my case, when I fully stepped into freelancing in advertising, a lot of my clients were looking to reach audiences I was used to reaching as a journalist. Yes, I had spent time honing my craft as a journalist but also my lived experience was an invaluable part of it as well. So when I told agencies about my experience, I didn't limit it to how long I'd been writing ads, but expanded it to include why my background made me a good fit to write what they were looking for. I wasn't only measuring my experience in length, but also measuring it in breadth.

VALUE OF YOUR TIME

Understanding the value of your time is, well, priceless. After I became a dad, my rate went up, plain and simple. One reason was because time spent on a project would be time away from my family, so it had to be worth it for me to take a gig. I understood that I might not get certain gigs because of my increased rate, and I was prepared for that because I truly valued my time with my family. Essentially I was 'busy.'

Being busy or not could be determined by what's going on in your life outside of work. How many gigs do you currently have? Would you just have been sitting on your couch? Do you have personal things planned ? Being clear about the climate of your life while considering your rate may help to bring you some clarity.

Think about where you are and what else could that time have gone to. If that time would have only been spent on the couch, there's a rate for that. If you could have been at the beach, there's a rate for that, too.

STATE OF THE MARKET

Knowing the industry standard in your field and at your level is always helpful in deciding on your rate. A few quick internet searches can give you some insight into some numbers that you can start to play with and possibly use as a base, so I won't spend a lot of time there. But if you are close enough to, and feel comfortable with them, ask a freelancer yourself.

Be mindful, though, that a lot of people are still very hush-hush and secretive about what they make. So it's key to approach someone you know that can shed some light on this still not so transparent area of the game. A friend or close colleague, if they feel comfortable, can give you a view from the ground level of what kind of money there is to be made in your field. Again, there's still a lot of controversy around money and disclosing numbers, which is why you should use your best judgment when broaching the subject.

But if you are able to have one of these Dollars Dialogues, it can save you a lot of time (and money) as you get into freelancing. I've been asked my rate by other freelancers I'm friends with and I've told them. I've also asked and people have told me. But everyone's different. The point is that one of these conversations can be valuable, and if you're fortunate enough to have someone share that with you, remember to pass it on.

A FEW WAYS YOU COULD APPROACH IT...

So you've gotten an average or an industry standard, cool. Now you need to figure out what your approach should be.

Option 1
You could come in right at the average, which is a reasonable and safe approach.

Option 2
You could be a little under if you're more concerned with staying booked and could possibly surpass those with high rates in total income.

Option 3
You could also go higher if you feel you deserve it or want to ensure that only certain gigs come your way.

—

Either way you go, knowing the going rate for your services, experience and skillset is an invaluable resource when setting your own rate.

TRUE PROFESSIONALS

SEEK PROFESSIONAL HELP

TIPS FROM THE TAX LADY

I can't take credit for this, because I've heard it several times from several people, but I definitely agree. When it comes to helping you with money and tax matters, find someone who cares about you. Yes, a competent professional could do a good enough job, but you really need to find someone who not only has your best interest at heart, but also is invested in your success in some way.

When I first started my career, I already knew who I was going to use to do my taxes. My best friend's mother, who's like a second mother to me, had always been "The Tax Lady." But growing up, I thought it was as simple as you bring her a W-2, she presses a few buttons on the computer and you get a refund check. I had no idea that as a freelancer I wouldn't be getting W-2's, wasn't usually gonna be getting a refund a lot of times or any of the other ways that freelance life affects you both mentally and financially. I was super green, but fortunately Valerie R. Clemons, E.A., C.P.A. of the Chicago-based Clemons and Associates, Inc. guided me through it.

With patience and care, she outlined how my career path was going to be different than a lot of my friends who were not self-employed, how to prepare for the costs ahead and how to put myself in the best position possible as a freelance creative. She gave me a lot of guidance as I navigated taxes, savings and how to shift my thinking into that of a business owner, not just a worker.

So it was only right that I brought in Mrs. Clemons for a little "freelance" help on this one. She and I had a conversation about some of the fundamental things people should keep in mind from a money, tax and mental perspective when getting into freelancing. The following pages are some of the highlights from that conversation, with seven tangible takeaways that can help any and all freelancers, new or old. So listen up, The Tax Lady's got something to say.

SAVE 30-50% OF WHAT YOU EARN

Knowing when and how to save money as a freelancer is beyond important. I can not stress enough how much of a learned and valuable skill this is. If you don't develop this skill, your career will either be very short or very chaotic, neither of which I endorse.

"How much and how you should save usually depends on how and why you became a freelancer," she explains. "There are two other terms that can apply here, which is independent contractor or just self-employed. They all mean that you're working for yourself. But a big thing to consider is, is this a side hustle or am I going in 100%? If you're going all in, it's very important. If it's a side hustle, technically you could not save at all."

While you could choose to hold your breath and just jump into the deep end, know that you'll still need to swim through these waters and will need to find a way to stay afloat at times.

IF YOU DON'T WANT TO STRUGGLE.

"Remember, you'll have taxes, fees and "rainy day" issues. If you're going all in, try to save half of what you have coming in. Taxes can be up to 30% of your income, so you should try to save 30%-50% if you don't want to struggle. A simple way to think about it is, every dollar you get, put a dollar aside."

TAX TIP #2

WRITE DOWN THE INS AND OUTS

In freelance, you'll need to learn how to manage your money. Mrs. Clemons stresses that this is essential and basic bookkeeping, which all freelancers will need to develop.

"It's important to write down all that is coming in and what is going out," she says. "There are also easy and inexpensive programs you can find from a quick internet search that are made for the non-accountant and can help you keep track of income and expenses."

KEEP TRACK OF INCOME AND EXPENSES.

She continues, "The most organized way is to have your bookkeeping system, and at the end of 1st quarter take a look at what your income and expenses are. That's the most efficient and least costly." This allows freelancers to forecast their money flow, understanding that this is not a perfect method and that different times of year will most likely net out different results.

TAX TIP #3

PLAN AHEAD

You'll also need to develop a sense of vision, or being able to look down the road and plan accordingly. This is key to keeping you on the right road financially and being ready for the common recurring expenses that come with the territory.

Mrs. Clemons advises that freelancers pay their taxes quarterly to avoid unnecessary penalties and fees. Understanding the ebbs and flows of income for freelancers, she understands that it may not be possible for everyone to just write a check to cover those taxes every three months. For those who may not have the cash on hand, "You may want to find a low-interest credit card and pay your taxes on that," she advises. "Also, look into getting a money manager. The money you save by consulting with them could cover their fees and then some."

IT MAY NOT BE POSSIBLE TO JUST WRITE A CHECK.

She also urges that freelancers talk to their CPA's before the end of the year. She says that early communication can help you steer your financial situation in the right direction. "You should reach out and have a conversation [with a CPA] around September or October so that we can look at the whole picture and advise you accordingly. Because after December 31st, we can't help you in that same way."

TAX TIP #4

GET YOUR FEELINGS & YOUR MIND RIGHT

A common and avoidable mistake that people make when first getting into freelancing, that may result in negative consequences for them in different ways, is not making some of the intangible shifts needed to succeed when you are your own business.

"Not preparing mentally and emotionally for the realities of freelance is one of the things I've seen over the years that has been problematic for people. When you have money in your hand, it's hard to let that go. That's why when you have a regular job, your employer takes [taxes, insurance, etc.] out for you. But you have to be prepared and remember that what you make, that's not all your money."

THAT'S NOT ALL YOUR MONEY.

She also emphasizes that while many want to concentrate on getting gigs and doing the work, you have to keep in mind that this is a business. If you want to hone in on a particular area, you might want to bring in others who can cover your blind spots.

"A lot of people, especially if you are in the arts or creative industries, like to put more of the focus on their talent or skill. That's okay, but then that means you need to put as much focus into finding someone that is trustworthy and responsible to help you get the money stuff right. It's not just taxes, it's also business expenses, living expenses, etc. It all boils down to planning and preparing."

TAX TIP #5

BOSS UP

While you can use freelance to generate some extra income, enter a new field or make a career change, this next tip is good for anyone to keep in mind, but especially for those going from working a full-time job to full-time freelancing. Pay close attention to this one.

STOP THINKING LIKE A WORKER.

"[With freelance] You're going from an employee to a business owner, and possible employer. You have to think of yourself as the 'boss of me and what I do'" she explains. "Whether you call it freelance, or an independent contractor or just self-employed, you decide when and how you work and how much to charge. At this point, you have to stop thinking like a worker."

TAX TIP #6

EASE INTO IT IF YOU CAN

Mrs. Clemons is a firm believer in working your way up to your goals, as opposed to dropping everything and making an immediate switch to freelance. She herself started her business by doing it part-time at first while she worked another job. Using that experience, she offers this.

"You might not be at the point where you're ready to quit your job, and that's fine. Something I heard and a simple way to think of it could be when your side hustle is paying as much as your day job, then it's probably time to quit your day job."

She advocates for saving up to a year's income (if you're able) before entering full on if you're looking to make this your main source of income. While this may or may not be right for your individual goals and personal situation, this is sage advice in an increasingly impatient world that usually champions instant gratification.

YOU MIGHT NOT BE READY TO QUIT YOUR JOB.

TAX TIP #7

ASK GOOD PEOPLE ABOUT GOOD PEOPLE

If you're looking to find a good CPA for your own business, Mrs. Clemons urges people to talk to those in their field and see who's working out for them.

90% COMES FROM WORD OF MOUTH.

"For our business, 90%, and it used to be 100%, comes from word of mouth," she explains. "We use a couple of services [to help our SEO] but it's really based on recommendations. Even in the pandemic, we've been fortunate to have people tell other people about us. There's a small degree of separation between clients sometimes and professionalism will always win."

So open up some dialogue with a few trusted friends or colleagues and see who they trust to get the job done. It will take you a long way.

IT DOESN'T HAVE TO BE TAXING.

ASKING FOR YOUR MONEY

WHEN TO ASK:
IF THE PAYMENT IS LATE.

HOW TO ASK:
RESPECTFULLY, THE WAY YOU'D WANT SOMEONE TO ASK YOU.

WHEN NOT TO ASK:
BEFORE INVOICE IS DUE.

But you can also negotiate those terms. Most agencies are Net-30, meaning they've got 30 days to pay you from when you submit your invoice, but depending on relationship you can negotiate. When taking on your own clients, you set the boundaries. It could be half up front, other half on completion. Or you could breakout weekly or biweekly pay for a longer project.

ON THE MONEY

There are a lot of details when it comes to money and yes, they can sometimes be overwhelming. But if you take away nothing else from the information in this section specifically, it should be to develop practices that serve you and how you work.

Everything doesn't work for everybody and one of your responsibilities as a freelancer, and as a business owner, is to be sure that you adhere to a model that allows you to succeed. It's not a science, it's really good habits, good people, good self-awareness and common sense at the end of the day.

CHAPTER 6

SELF INVESTMENT

I don't think there is a single piece of information that I'm trying to get across to you that's more important than this. No business can be successful if there is no investment in that business and the tools and resources that business needs to thrive. Since you are your business, that means investing in you.

If you ask any business owner, they'll tell you that investment comes before you see a return, so it's important for you to understand this, too. Freelancing can be a hustle, a quick way to make some extra money, and there's nothing wrong with that. But if you intend on playing the long game, there is no way of getting around the importance of self investment.

3 KEY WAYS:

TIME
ENERGY
FINANCES

TIME.

There's no more important resource because it's the one that you can't get back. This makes it inherently valuable so you should spend it with that same value in mind.

We live in a quick-turn, one-day delivery type of culture which sometimes makes it hard to see the value in spending real time on your craft, skill or business. And I'm gonna be straight up with you- that's the quickest way to become a hack.

Those that make a living performing under these quick-turn conditions can do so because they've put in the time to be able to quickly perform when needed. It's a great idea to spend as many hours as necessary researching, studying, practicing, sketching, writing, learning color theory, even worrying (so that you can get it out and over with and be able to move forward with confidence.) Whatever your field or discipline, immerse yourself in it, continually. Know the new ways of communicating, the new rules that govern your industry and just continue to get better. This will always be true and valuable at any point in your freelance journey.

ENERGY.

Putting your energy towards meeting your goals—and using that energy efficiently—is another critical investment. That encompasses networking (whether in-person or virtually), emailing, making schedules and lists, developing routines, self-reflection and self-inventory. Anything that provides clarity, builds relationships, creates infrastructure or generally adds to you and your business are good uses of your energy.

But you don't have to do them all at once or the way that other people are doing them. For instance, there are certain platforms I use to promote myself and my business and others I don't. I don't try to "be everywhere" because for me that's exhausting, I'm generally uninterested and it is not my personal business model. But it does work for some people and for colleagues and friends of mine. It's up to you to decide the most fruitful avenues to allow your energy to travel down.

FINANCES.

A common phrase comes to mind, "it takes money to make money." This is true. But it doesn't have to take a lot of money up front to do this. Look at anything that will help you develop, learn or sharpen a skill, become inspired or help expand your network as a worthy financial investment.

That includes classes, books (like this one, wink), videos, software, coffee dates, dinners, equipment, therapy, whatever. If these things will contribute to you and your business becoming more successful, these seem like smart buys.

If you're not working with a lot of money, please don't be discouraged. This only means you may need to be more judicious about the money you do have to spend and being more resourceful to bridge the gaps. The beginning of my freelance career was built on using computers at local libraries because I couldn't afford internet at home. Where there's a will…you know the rest.

WHAT DO TIME, ENERGY & MONEY NEED TO NOT BE WASTED?

FOCUS.

Have a reason for each of the things you invest in. It doesn't need to be a deep soliloquy, it just needs to be true to you and your vision as a freelancer. Yes, there is something to be said for just being in the right place at the right time. And also something to be said for doing everything you can, being at every event and making yourself available as well. But focus attached to these investments means that you are intentionally setting yourself apart from your peers. Focus up and you'll continue to mindfully build the path towards your goals.

ONE LAST THING...

No matter how your first gig goes, keep going. Whether you did amazing, horrible, aight or anywhere in between, go after the next one. This is a marathon and however you feel at mile one, use that to get to mile two.

GOING.

It went great? Boom, that's momentum and confidence that you can ride to get you that next gig.

Not so great? It happens. Take some of the money you made and treat yourself, reflect, and get ready to jump back in.

PART 3: **AFTER THE GIG**

JOB, WELL... DONE?

You did it.

You successfully completed your first freelance gig. You've just started another career, side hustle, back up plan or whatever you want freelancing to be for you. You should definitely celebrate and mark this milestone.

And you definitely shouldn't think that just because the gig is over that means the work is done.

Nah, this is the necessary overtime that comes with freelancing. Its making sure that your i's are dotted and your t's are crossed. Tying up loose ends and hopefully making your way to a few more ends. The point is, there are a few things that you still need to do, even after the job is done, to make sure that you enjoy the fruits of your labor. Oh, and be on the way to that next gig.

CHAPTER 7

C.L.O.S.E. IT OUT RIGHT

The way you end the gig is extremely important. It's the last thing people remember. The final impression and sometimes the most lasting. So take control of it by making sure you do everything in your power to finish up like a true professional. This is how you can become a successful *Closer.*

C —— heck Your Boxes
L —— ook Back on The Process
O —— wn the Outcome
S —— ew Seeds For New Relationships
E —— xit Like You Enter

CHECK YOUR BOXES

Invoice

Send your final invoices as soon as you've completed the gig so that there's no delay in your payments.

Final Deliverables

Be sure to send layered files, final documents, finished decks or any other pieces that you were tasked with creating as part of your agreement.

Return Equipment

If you were lent a computer, phone, prototype or any other materials that allowed you to effectively do your job, be sure to return them promptly. No one wants to have to ask for their stuff back, so be mindful there.

L.

LOOK BACK ON THE PROCESS

What happened?

Try to first think about this in facts, i.e. the campaign that I worked on wasn't chosen, before thinking about it as a conclusion, i.e. the campaign I was working on wasn't chosen because the work wasn't good enough. This is key to more accurately evaluating a gig in hindsight. We are all storytellers by nature, with our minds filling the gaps and helping to bring us to a certain understanding of things. But before we tell the story, take note of the events as clearly as you can. This will be very important in deciding what's working in the present, how you can improve in the future and if you want to continue working with a colleague or client going forward.

I used to give my 100% on a project and as soon as it was done, put it in my rear view. I had gotten what I need from it, or so I thought, and was ready to move on to the next. It wasn't until I started to have these personal project debriefings that I started to see patterns, wins I wasn't even paying attention to, ways that I was making other people's jobs harder and other things that I was able to act upon after reflecting. The best freelancer is a self aware one, and taking inventory in this way can get you closer to being your best.

What did you learn?

No matter if it's the shittiest of shitty gigs, there is always something to learn from each and every one. Sometimes it could be a new skill, a new program, learning that you're not as good a communicator as you thought or learning that you never want to freelance at a particular company again. There is a lesson to be learned with every gig experience, and the more you're able to observe and act on these lessons, the better you'll get at this freelance thing.

What would you change?

It's not about what was done wrong, there's no value judgment in this question. It could very well be something you felt was done wrong if that language is true to you, but it's more about how you, your process, ways of working and perspectives can shift. It could be as simple as I would have presented the work this way instead of that way, or I would have managed my time better. Be kind to yourself. It shouldn't be a harsh process. The point is to shed light on ways that you can switch up your approach to have better success in the future.

It can also be helpful to go through this exercise with someone else who worked on the project with you. They'll be able to present a different perspective and possibly show you some things that you would not have been able to see on your own.

How did you grow?

There are a lot of ways that you can grow from a gig; financially, through contacts and connections gained, work produced, etc. Being as open as possible with your definition of growth can also help you when asking yourself these questions. For instance, you may have grown in a way you may not be paying attention to because your attention may be going to what's a little bit easier to see. You may have been asked to work on a pitch project where you lost the pitch but found a new creative partner. Try to look at it from as many angles as you can to identify some of the "new growth" you might not have noticed.

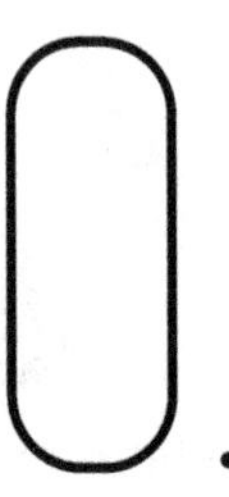

OWN THE OUTCOME

Accountability Is Key

From what was made to how it was handled. Own it. That doesn't mean taking responsibility for things that were out of your hands. It means accepting what happened, how it happened and your part in it.

That could mean celebrating your great ideas that helped push a campaign over the top, or being real about some places where you could or should have done better. Projects can switch and morph and evolve into something completely different in the end from where they started. That means a lot of shifts, conversations, responsibilities, restrictions and a million other things may have changed along the way. Being both real and fair with yourself about the final output is key to developing self awareness and an awareness of who and what it takes for a project to be successful.

S.

SEW SEEDS FOR NEW RELATIONSHIPS

Exchange Info

Think of it like you're back in high school and every gig is the end of the year. Have people sign your yearbook, or more plainly stated, exchange contact info so that you can stay in touch.

Whether that's portfolio sites, social media handles, phone numbers or the like, be proactive about solidifying the new connections you're making. And be sure to follow up or check up on them periodically to keep the lines of communication open. Your relationships are one of if not your most valuable asset in freelancing.

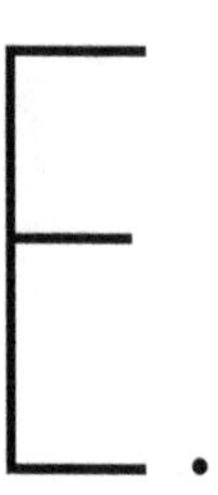

EXIT LIKE YOU ENTER

Work Your Last Day Like Your First

No slacking at the end. Bring that same energy, enthusiasm and contribution to the project until the very last moment. Even if it was a rough one, personal consistency says a lot about you and what you bring to the table, so stay true to that first day attitude.

Leave a Great Impression

Write a thank you note, let your team know how you've learned from them, send a card of appreciation. And if none of these expressions are true to your personality, that's cool too. But find a way to express sincerity and gratitude for the opportunity.

Be a True Professional

You may have worked with some difficult personalities, or even not have been given the tools you needed to succeed. This will happen. But don't lose your cool or spaz on anybody when it's over. In essence, don't let anyone take you outside of your character.

DON'T FORGET TO FOLLOW UP

Tracking Down Work: As a freelancer it's important to keep updating your book with your latest and greatest work. So you'll need to make sure you follow up with your project lead or contact to get finished versions of your work for your portfolio. You may need to be persistent about this, as the responses after the gig can come in a lot slower than responses during. But be diligent and remember that it's up to you to make sure you get what you need.

Let Avails Be Known: If you enjoyed working with someone, let them know that you are open to doing it again and what your schedule may be looking like in the near future. It's good to be clear about your intentions and give tangible reasons to stay on their minds.

Referrals: It could also be good, especially if you're just starting, to ask for referrals from clients, partners and teams that you've worked well with. It's a way to build your reputation and let others know how you handle yourself in the freelance space. If you think this would be valuable for your practice, don't be afraid to ask for it.

IN CLOSING...

WELCOME TO THE

So now you've been initiated. You're a freelancer, a business owner and a vital part of what is called the Gig Economy. Now comes the responsibility to build, to learn, to challenge yourself and to lend a hand to others in the name of community who are also looking to follow in these same footsteps.

GIG ECONOMY.

I continue to stand on the shoulders and in the legacy of my Ancestors, friends, colleagues and collaborators who have all added to me and my knowledge base. I thank them tremendously and you, too, for coming on the journey with me through this book. I hope the very best for you and your practice as you continue this journey on your own.